Basic Domestic Pet Library

Kingsnakes & Milk Snakes
A Complete and Up-to-Date Guide

J.E. Smith

Published in association with T.F.H. Publications, Inc.,
the world's largest and most respected publisher of pet literature

Chelsea House Publishers
Philadelphia

Basic Domestic Pet Library

A Cat in the Family
Amphibians Today
Aquarium Beautiful
Choosing the Perfect Cat
Dog Obedience Training
Dogs: Selecting the Best Dog for You
Ferrets Today
Guppies Today
Hamsters Today
Housebreaking and Training Puppies
Iguanas in Your Home
Kingsnakes & Milk Snakes
Kittens Today
Lovebirds Today
Parakeets Today
Pot-bellied Pigs
Rabbits Today
Turtles Today

Publisher's Note: All of the photographs in this book have been coated with FOTO-GLAZE® finish, a special lamination that imparts a new dimension of colorful gloss to the photographs.

Reinforced Library Binding & Super-Highest Quality Boards

This edition © T.F.H. Publications, Inc., 1 TFH Plaza, Neptune City, NJ 07753. This special library bound edition is made expressly for Chelsea House Publishers, a division of Main Line Book Company.

1 3 5 7 9 8 6 4 2

Library of Congress Cataloging-in-Publication Data

KING & MILK SNAKES

A QUESTION & ANSWER yearBOOK

by J. E. Smith

There is little doubt as to the enormous popularity of the king and milk snakes. They are among the most sough-after and commonly bred snakes in the world. They are colorful, easy to keep, a breeze to breed, and make wonderful herpetological conversation pieces.

The need for clear, concise, and reliable information on just about any popular topic is always an urgent one. Plenty of people keep and breed king and milk snakes, but how many of those same people write about it? There literally are *thousands* of snake-keepers out there who have scores of unanswered questions banging on the walls of their mind. Their curiosities are limitless, and yet the answers they require, sadly, often are far and few between.

In the pages ahead, experienced keeper J. E. Smith will attempt to answer many commonly asked questions about king and milk snakes, delving into such vital topics as feeding, breeding, acquiring, housing, and tending to health problems. The unique question-and-answer format was designed to make matters both simple and enjoyable—read this book like you would a novel. If you come across a question you already know the answer to, skip over it. By the time you turn the last page, most of the mysteries that have plagued you for so long should be long gone.

I hope you enjoy reading this book half as much as I enjoyed preparing it for publication.

by W. P. Mara, Editor

What are YearBOOKs?

Because keeping snakes as pets is growing at a rapid pace, information on their selection, care, and breeding is vitally needed in the marketplace. Books, the usual way information of this sort is transmitted, can be too slow. Sometimes by the time a book is written and published, the material contained therein is a year or two old...and no new material has been added during that time. Only a book in a magazine form can bring breaking stories and current information. A magazine is streamlined in production, so we have adopted certain magazine publishing techniques in the creation of this yearBOOK. Magazines also can be much cheaper than books because they are supported by advertising. To combine these assets into a great publication, we issued this yearBOOK in both magazine and book format at different prices.

yearBOOKS, INC.
Glen S. Axelrod
Chief Executive Officer

Mark Johnson
*Vice President Sales
& Marketing*
Barry Duke
Chief Operating Officer

Neil Pronek
Katherine J. Carlon
Managing Editors

DIGITAL PRE-PRESS
Ken Pecca
Supervisor

John Palmer
Jose Reyes
Digital Pre-Press Production

Computer Art
Patti Escabi
Candida Moreira
Michele Newcomer

Advertising Sales
Nancy S. Rivadeneira
Advertising Sales Director
Chris O'Brien
Advertising Account Manager
Jennifer Johnson
Advertising Coordinator
Adrienne Rescinio
*Advertising Production
Coordinator*
c yearBOOKS, Inc.
1 TFH Plaza
Neptune City, NJ 07753
Completely Manufactured in
Neptune City, NJ USA

CONTENTS

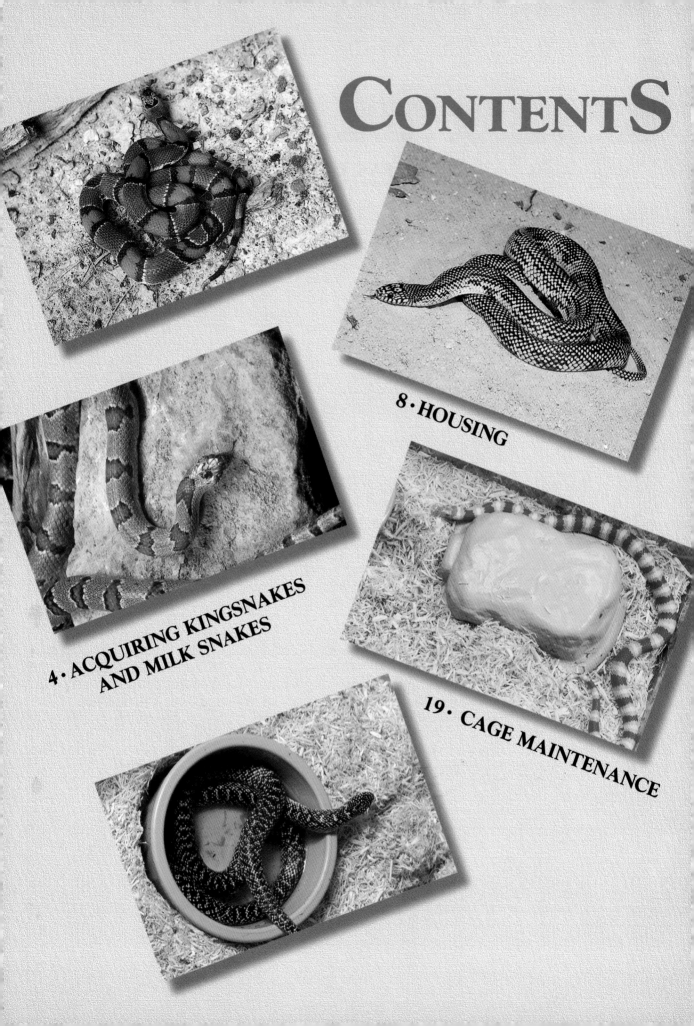

8 · HOUSING

4 · ACQUIRING KINGSNAKES
AND MILK SNAKES

19 · CAGE MAINTENANCE

39 · BREEDING

21 · FEEDING

34 · COMMON DISEASES

ACQUIRING KINGSNAKES AND MILK SNAKES

Q: Where can I get top-quality specimens?

There are a number of places the interested person can go for high-quality king and milk snake specimens these days—that is one of the beneficial side-effects of the herpetological hobby's current popularity. The most obvious place is in a pet store. Since there is so much captive breeding going on, chances are any specimen you see will not be wild-caught (except in the case of some adults.) You should keep in mind that you will be paying a full retail price on store-bought snakes, but most stores have a short-term return policy if anything goes wrong, and of course the convenience of a shop being nearby is hard to match.

Q: Can king and milk snake specimens be taken from the wild?

They can be, but they definitely should not be. There are a number of reasons why. First, the moral issue. We live in a very conservation-minded age, and the laws that protect wild animals

King and milk snakes are among the most popular snakes in the world. This isn't too hard to understand when you see specimens like these two dazzling Queretaro (also sometimes called Ruthven's) Kingsnakes, *Lampropeltis ruthveni*. (The lighter specimen is an albino). Photo by Isabelle Francais.

are getting stricter and stricter. Ignoring these laws hurts everyone. Countless local governments, not just in the United States but globally, have literally been forced into designing laws to protect their native species. Many governments tried to do it the "understanding" way first, by giving hobbyists

has already happened with a large number of creatures, reptiles and amphibians among them, and such tragedies will only increase if we keep turning to wild populations simply to nurture our collections.

Second, along similar lines, there are legal penalties to consider. Now more than ever we are seeing violators

anyway. They are in better shape, they are better in temperament, and 99 times out of 100 they will eat without fuss. That is something you can never guarantee with a wild-caught animal. There's so much captive-breeding going on nowdays anyway that it's not even financially beneficial to take wild specimens.

Most king and milk snakes eat rodents, but some have a stubborn drive to eat only other reptiles (including other snakes). Unless you have access to a steady flow of these creatures, buy only kings and milks that prove a willingness to eat mice and rats. Photo of a San Luis Potosi Kingsnake, *Lampropeltis mexicana*, by Isabelle Francais.

some leeway, but in the end those privileges were abused to the point where the drawing up of regulations was the only choice left.

The truth is, like it or not, if we continue to abuse our wild populations they will simply disappear. This

paying stiff fines and even serving prison time for their ecological offenses. Many people think the possibility of this happening is a joke, but it is not. It is very much a reality.

Finally, captive-bred specimens are far superior to wild ones

Q: Are king and milk snakes expensive?

It depends on the exact snake in question, but some can be, especially if you are purchasing a captive-bred, sexually mature adult of a rare species or subspecies, for example.

Q: If I have to have a snake shipped to me, will it be expensive?

It certainly can be. In the United States there is a law prohibiting snakes from being shipped through the "standard" mail system.

fifty dollars. Often, however, a dealer will split this cost with you, or, if you happen to know anyone who is also buying from the same dealer, you can ship multiple snakes in the same package and

Start with the eyes and the mouth—these are often the locations for the first signs of ill-health. Are the rims of the eyes clear, or are they puffy and watery? Does the mouth close easily or does it hang open just slightly as if the snake has trouble closing it? Let the snake move about freely in your hand for a moment or two. How are its movements? Does it seem listless or lively? A sick snake will seem sluggish whereas a healthy one will probably try to get away (hatchlings are notoriously energetic.) If the snake

Most king and milk snakes are relatively affordable, but some of the 'choicer' varieties can be fairly expensive. Adult examples of the beautiful Gray-banded Kingsnake, *Lampropeltis alterna*, for example, usually are very costly. Photo by William B. Allen, Jr.

In fact, the only legal way to ship a snake, venomous or nonvenomous, is by air freight. Even the lightest package containing a snake will run at least

divide the freight costs among yourselves.

Q: What should I look for when inspecting a king or milk snake that I'm thinking about buying?

feels like a length of lifeless rope in your hand, perhaps it isn't the one you should buy. Also, how does it feel weight-wise? This will of course be an instinctive

Photo of a California Kingsnake, *Lampropeltis getula californiae*, by Isabelle Francais.

guess, but there are visual clues as well. Does the animal look as though it has been eating or does its skin hang loosely from its body? Also, don't be afraid to ask the seller if you can actually see the animal eat—there is nothing wrong with wanting some assurance on your investment.

Photo of a Gray-banded Kingsnake, *Lampropeltis alterna*, by Isabelle Francais.

One argument for buying adult *Lampropeltis* specimens is that they almost always are willing and eager feeders. Also, adults can immediately be used as breeding stock. Photo of a Gray-banded Kingsnake, *Lampropeltis alterna*, by Isabelle Francais.

HOUSING

THE TANK

Q: What size tank will a king or milk snake need?

Snakes of the genus *Lampropeltis* don't grow all that large, so a keeper will probably never need a tank any bigger than a 30-gallon 'long' per adult pair. The longest member of this group attains a length of around four to four and a half feet and will not be much thicker than the diameter of a 50-cent piece.

Q: Should I use a glass tank with king and milk snakes or can I build one from wood?

A commonly asked question. While it is perfectly understandable for a keeper to want to design their own tank from wood, I would have to say in the long run glass is infinitely better because king and milk snakes really don't need all that much room in the first place, it is much more convenient to simply go out and purchase a tank as opposed to having to go through the trouble of building one. The most important reason of all, however, is that glass tanks can be scrubbed clean whereas a similar

When a snake refuses food, sometimes the problem lies not in its health but in its housing. Environment has a stronger effect on a captive snake's behavior than many people realize. Photo of a San Luis Potosi Kingsnake, *Lampropeltis mexicana*, by Isabelle Francais.

level of cleanliness is impossible to obtain with wood. Of course, a keeper can take the middle road to this issue and build a tank out of glass. The problem is, this is a very tedious and time-consuming process that many will find more stressful than rewarding.

drafts (which you shouldn't) the standard quarter-inch hardware cloth wire tops, purchased at any pet store that sells tanks, will do the job just fine. If you have a tankful of newborns then perhaps you may want to consider acquiring something a

the quarter-inch hardware cloth tops with fine mesh screening.

Q: How can I secure the top I use?
There are a number of ways, but the simplest is to buy "tank clips," which come in two general shapes—round and

Glass tanks, purchased at a pet shop, are infinitely better for king and milk snakes than wooden enclosures built at home. Glass is easier to clean and lasts longer. Also, glass will better tolerate little mishaps like spilled water. Photo of a Blotched Kingsnake, *Lampropeltis getula goini*, by R. D. Bartlett.

ENCLOSURE COMPONENTS

Q: What's the best type of tank top to use with king and milk snakes?
Unless you are putting your snakes in a room where there are cold

little 'tighter,' since neonatal *Lampropeltis* are so tiny they can easily squeeze through the aforementioned quarter-inch screen. One solution to this problem utilized by keepers is the practice of covering the inside of

square. The round type are nothing more than small steel curls with a great amount of tension. These are slipped under the plastic rim of a tank then snapped onto the tops. They are fairly inexpensive and widely available.

The square clips attach to the top and tank in the same fashion and are usually made of a thin but sturdy aluminum or steel. These too simply snap into place, are inexpensive, and widely available. They are also slightly easier to work with than the

climbers although they are perfectly capable of climbing and do so very well.

Q: What size water bowl will I need?

A fairly small one. Kingsnakes and milk snakes are not avid swimmers and will not lay in a water bowl like a

opening so the snakes will not be able to tip it over.

Q: Do king and milk snakes need a lot of rocks?

Not really. In essence, all they really need is one—to use as a starting point when they begin to shed. When the appropriate time comes,

Most snakes are naturally gifted escape artists, so their enclosures must be well-secured. The last thing you want to do is lose a beautiful (and probably quite expensive) specimen like this breathtaking albino Queretaro Kingsnake, *Lampropeltis ruthveni*. Photo by Isabelle Francais.

aforementioned "curly clips."

Q: Will a king or milk snake need a branch to climb on?

You might as well put one in. Members of this genus are not frequent

garter snake or a water snake. The bowl can be about four inches (10.1 cm) in diameter and filled with only about an inch of water. The base of the bowl should be wider in diameter than the

they will rub their snouts against the abrasive surface until the old skin begins to come loose. Kingsnakes and milk snakes also like to curl up behind rocks and use them as hiding places as well, so you will afford them an extra measure of security and shelter with each one you include.

Q: Do kingsnakes and milk snakes need hideboxes?

Most definitely. As much as we would like to believe they enjoy being out in the open where we can see them, kingsnakes and milk snakes place a great value on privacy. There are indeed some snakes that seem perfectly at ease in tanks where they are exposed all the time, but members of this genus prefer to have dark, secure hiding places nearby in case they feel the need to retreat.

Q: How can I supply my snake(s) with an effective hidebox?

Actually, the easiest way is often the least expensive. Remember, the key to a good hidebox is that it gives the occupant a true sense of security, serenity, and isolation. You can make hideboxes out of just about anything. Some keepers make them out of old cardboard boxes, which they then dispose of and replace, while others build hideboxes from scratch using pieces of plywood. You can go a step further by purchasing dark-colored

Most king and milk snakes need a moderate-sized waterbowl, not because they need lots of drinking water, but because they often like to sit in the water to bathe or loosen their old skin prior to shedding. Photo of a Desert Kingsnake, *Lampropeltis getula splendida*, by Isabelle Francais.

plastic food containers and drilling a large hole in the lid (these can also be used again and again) or, if you're really ambitious and want something that looks natural, you can make one using stones and cement.

Q: What's the best type of cage bedding to use with king snakes and milk snakes?

That depends on your needs. If you are not concerned with the laborious process of carrying and cleaning a heavy tank, then aquarium gravel is a fine

The best type of bedding to use with king and milk snakes is a matter of personal choice. Some keepers go for very simple items such as paper towels or newspapers, others like naturalistic beddings, like the moss bed shown with this Guatemalan Milk Snake, *Lampropeltis triangulum abnorma*. Photo by Isabelle Francais.

choice. You should always use a heavier grade rather than a finer one because you always run the risk of a snake ingesting small pieces along with its food item in the case of the latter. One advantage gravel has to it is that it can be used over and over again. Also, a tank set up with the correctly color-coordinated gravel can be very attractive. Gravel is not terribly expensive and can be found in virtually every pet store around.

Many hobbyists like to use wood shavings,

although they tend to be very messy and don't do much for the tank's visual appeal. While it's true they are inexpensive and can be bought in huge quantities, they can also harm your snake—sharp slivers can stick to a food item, get swallowed, and actually puncture the snake's stomach or intestinal wall.

Pine bark nuggets and pine bark mulch are also commonly used. They are, like the wood shavings, inexpensive and can be bought in

bulk. The only problem to watch for here is that pine bark mulch and nuggets are ideal breeding grounds for mites and ticks. Even if your snake does not have any of these nasty ectoparasites, the mulch and the nuggets might (although bags purchased from pet shops rather than garden supply centers almost always are 'clean').

Indoor/outdoor carpeting is also very popular. In short, it is a sheet of "fake turf" cut to fit the floor dimensions of your tank. The advantages to a sheet of indoor/outdoor carpeting are obvious—you can reuse it time and time again, it is easy to clean, and it actually looks kind of nice. However, a keeper should be made aware that after a short amount of time this stuff really begins to smell horrible—no matter how hard you try to wash it, at some point the odor of snake waste will seem permanently absorbed. Also, mites and ticks seem to think indoor/outdoor carpeting makes a wonderful home.

Getting away from visual aesthetics and going strictly for economy, one could always give newspaper a try. There are both good and bad sides to using it. On the good side, newspaper certainly is inexpensive and easy enough to work with. One could conceivably afford to clean their tank every day whether it needed it or not. For keepers who have many king and milk snakes, such an approach is very sensible. The bad point, however,

Wood shavings are a very popular cage bedding. Wood shavings are easy to work with, fairly natural in appearance, and can be purchased at most pet shops. Photo of a California Kingsnake, *Lampropeltis getula californiae*, by Isabelle Francais.

Four Paws offers a wide range of heat sources for your reptiles—heated rocks and caves for the interior of your tank, and undertank heaters which warm the entire habitat. Photo courtesy of Four Paws.

is that some herp hobbyists have claimed their snakes have bad reactions to the ink.

Finally, simple paper toweling is a route chosen by many of the more serious keepers who are not particularly interested in natural appearance. Although I am not personally fond of such a "clinical" look, I must say paper towels do seem to offer much—they are very sanitary (and thus harmless to your snakes), easy to remove and replace, and can be bought in bulk at a very cheap price.

CLIMATE CONTROL

Q: What's the best ambient temperature for king and milk snakes?

It depends mostly on where the animal is naturally from, but an acceptable temperature gradient is usually between 75 and 85°F— this of course referring to the time of year when the

Keeping an eye on the ambient temperature and humidity of your king and/or milk snakes' tank is an important facet of good husbandry. High-range thermometers and hygrometers designed specifically for herp-keeping are now available. Photo courtesy of Ocean Nutrition.

snake is considered "active." Desert-dwelling species can be kept at the higher end of this spectrum (the temperature being lowered slightly during the night hours) and the more northerly ranging specimens at the lower end.

Q: What's the best way to heat a snake's tank?

There are a number of methods at the keeper's disposal. The first and most obvious is simply to keep it in a room that's already heated. Even during the winter months there will (hopefully) be a part of every house that has enough heat to comfortably sustain a snake that is not being hibernated.

Another method is to use an item known as a "hot rock." In short, a hot rock is nothing more than a small piece of concrete that was poured around a heating element. When plugged in, the "rock" will reach a temperature of about 85 to 90°F. The advantages to having one of these include the fact that a snake can slither off it whenever it feels overheated, and hot rocks usually don't cost much to purchase or operate. It should be pointed out, however, that in order to operate a hot rock you will have to

By providing a basking spot for your king and milk snakes and then leaving the rest of the enclosure relatively cool, you let the snakes decide where they want to be. Photo of a Gray-banded Kingsnake, *Lampropeltis alterna*, by Isabelle Francais.

run the cord over the rim of the tank, which means the top will not be able to close completely. This of course compromises tank security. Furthermore, hot rocks cannot get wet.

A third method of tank heating involves the use of an undertank heating pad. In essence, the commercial heating pads sold specifically for use with reptile and amphibian tanks are simple sheets of heavy-duty rubber with power lines running through them. They have one adhesive side that is supposed to be stuck to the bottom of a snake's tank. When plugged in, the pads will reach about 95°F, warming that particular spot of the tank floor. These pads are relatively inexpensive and are quite useful, but the keeper may be annoyed at the fact that the pad is permanently stuck to the bottom of the tank. Therefore, it is advised that it be wrapped in tin foil before its first use, then simply slipped under the tank at the spot desired. As with the hot rock, the snake only has a particular "warm zone" that can be abandoned at any time.

Finally, "spot" heating is often used in modern herpetoculture, although it is mainly used with lizards. It involves the use of a heat lamp, which is nothing more than a lamp with a heating bulb. These bulbs are fairly inexpensive and can be purchased at most pet or horticultural stores. The problem is sometimes the lamps will produce so much heat that the entire tank will warm up too much and the snake(s) will not be able escape into a cooler area if it wishes to. Thus, it is best

King and milk snakes need an average daytime temperature of about 75 to 85°F/24 to 30°C, depending on where they occur geographically. Those from more southerly regions usually need higher temperatures. Photo of a San Luis Potosi Kingsnake, *Lampropeltis mexicana*, by Isabelle Francais.

to keep the lamp at a reasonable distance from the spot you wish to heat and to be cautious in its use.

Q: I understand full-spectrum lighting is needed with other reptiles. Is it also needed with king and milk snakes?

No, but studies have suggested that snakes exposed to full-spectrum lighting during the breeding season produce better results. The general answer to the question, no, refers to the fact that snakes, unlike lizards and turtles, do not need daily exposure to full-spectrum lighting in order to survive, but it is generally believed that a keeper will get better results from a breeding pair if they are in contact with this type of light. A period of about four to six hours of full-spectrum lighting per day is all that's needed, then once eggs have been laid, it is no longer necessary.

Q: Do I need to keep a king or milk snake's tank moist and humid?

No. Members of this genus occur in relatively dry areas. There are some subspecies that occur in tropical climates, but even these can be kept with the moisture at a minimum. A light daily misting of the tank is more than enough for these forms.

Q: How much ventilation do king and milk snakes need?

Not much. It is generally believed that snakes, like people, need lots of oxygen. This is untrue. There have been many examples of snakes being kept in containers

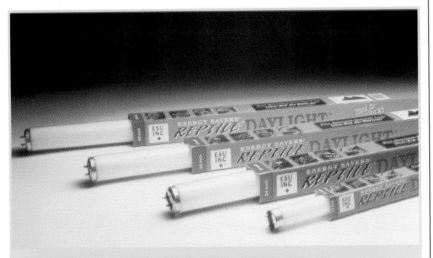

Providing your king and milk snakes with the correct photoperiod (day/night cycle) is very important. Bulbs designed specifically for the keeping of reptiles and amphibians now are available at many pet shops. Photo courtesy of Energy Savers.

with tops that were completely solid, allowing virtually no air to pass at all. Indeed, when snakes are shipped through the mail it is often in airtight packaging for a full day or two. Most tank tops are made from hardware cloth or aluminum screening and allow the free passage of air to begin with, which of course does them no harm, but if you feel your king or milk snake is in a cage that does not permit enough air circulation, simply lift the lid once every day and let the tank "air out" for a few moments.

It should be mentioned, however, that if a snake of any kind is left in a room that is prone to cold drafts, it will be very easy for the snake to develop a respiratory infection. Snakes are particularly susceptible to ailments of this kind, and cool breezes are undoubtedly a chief cause. Thus, over-ventilation can be just as much of a danger, if not a greater one, than the opposite.

Keeping a snake's tank clean is one of the most important parts of efficient husbandry. Photo of a Gray-banded Kingsnake, *Lampropeltis alterna*, by Isabelle Francais.

CAGE MAINTENANCE

Q: How often does a king or milk snake's tank need to be given a really thorough cleaning?

Ideally speaking, every time a snake defecates, the tank should be cleaned, but sometimes simply cleaning up the dirtied spot is sufficient (temporarily of course). In the long run, however, a king or milk snake's tank should be given a thorough and vigorous cleaning every ten days to two weeks.

Q: What is the best method for thoroughly cleaning a king or milk snake's tank?

First, remove the occupants. It is simply impossible to function with snakes lacing themselves around your arms or slithering out onto the floor. Take them out and place them in a secure temporary container. A bucket with a locking lid is a good choice. Next, remove all implements from the tank, such as branches,

hot rocks, etc., until the tank is stripped bare (although certain substrates, like gravel, will obviously remain.) Keep the reusable implements in one container (again, a bucket is good) and dispose of the rest.

Now it is time to wash the tank. The most effective solution is a mixture of warm water, soap, and a small amount of bleach. The soap is responsible for

A king or milk snake's tank should be attended to every time the animal defecates. Thorough and complete cleanings should be performed every ten to 14 days. Photo of a Pueblan Milk Snake, *Lampropeltis triangulum campbelli*, by William B. Allen, Jr.

Snake tanks can be cleaned with water, soap, and a little bleach, but make sure the tank is thoroughly rinsed out afterwards. A snake's skin will not take kindly to bleach residue. Photo of an Eastern Chain Kingsnake, *Lampropeltis getula getula*, by Mark Smith.

the general cleaning of dirt, and the bleach kills off the germs. Many keepers have expressed concern over the use of something as harsh as bleach, but I have never had any of my own snakes suffer adverse effects from it. The key is to use it sparingly.

Scrub the tank with a soft sponge rather than something abrasive. The reason is obvious—you will scratch the glass. Even the filthiest tanks will come clean eventually. Be sure to give special attention to the corners because this is where the germs will

be missed most easily. As for reusable substrates like rocks, simply let the soapy mixture run through it and churn with your hand at the same time until the effluent runs clear. Rinse the tank (and the possible substrate) with cold water and be sure you do it very thoroughly. This is perhaps the most important step in the procedure since neglecting it can cause potential harm to your captives.

When the tank is completely rinsed, wash and rinse all cage

implements in the same fashion, dry everything off thoroughly, then set the cage back up again. Finally, if you wish, you can also give the snakes themselves a bath, but only in warm water (no bleach and no soap) and dry them off completely immediately afterward. To some people, giving a snake a bath might seem kind of silly, but the truth is most captive snakes can really benefit from it. They lay in a dirty tank from time to time and their skins certainly don't clean themselves.

FEEDING

FOOD ITEMS

Q: What food items do king and milk snakes most often accept?

Members of the genus *Lampropeltis* can be expected to regularly accept either small mammals or reptiles—including other snakes. Other items have been recorded, including birds, insects, frogs and toads, various eggs, etc., but for the most part a king or milk snake will show the most interest in a mouse, rat, lizard, or other snake.

Q: Where can I obtain food items for king and milk snakes?

There are a number of places. In the case of obtaining reptiles as food items, you may find yourself in a difficult position. Since reptiles are generally sold as pets in the first place you will probably end up paying through the nose to maintain a king or a milk snake that only wants to eat little snakes or lizards. Some animal distributors and a few breeders are sympathetic to this cause and keep large numbers of skinks and small snakes (like brown snakes or garter snakes, for example) in stock, but even then you can suffer heavy financial setbacks. If you happen to live in a warm climate where reptiles are abundant and legal to catch, you can always collect your own. But in truth, a king or a milk snake that only eats other reptiles is going to be trouble.

Speaking in terms of mice and rats, try a pet store. As with the obtaining of the snakes

Most king and milk snakes are voracious eaters, so any prospective keeper should be prepared for the expense of a considerable food bill. Photo of a San Luis Potosi Kingsnake, *Lampropeltis mexicana*, by Isabelle Francais.

Frozen (and neatly packaged) rodents now are available for the keeper who has trained his or her snakes to take pre-killed food items. See your local pet shop about the availability of such products. Photo courtesy of Ocean Nutrition.

themselves, this is the most convenient option. Mice and rats are sold by virtually every pet store that sells herptiles. A good pet store will stock mice and rats of all different sizes, from newborn pups (rats) and pinkies (mice) to full-adult breeders. Also, most pet shops these days offer both live and frozen rodents.

FEEDING TIME

Q: Is it better to offer a king or milk snake live food or dead food?

This is a question that has certainly gotten a lot of attention in the herp hobby. Most professional

keepers would say dead food is better. Logically, the idea of giving a king or a milk snake its meals in a state where they won't have to work for it sounds very appealing— the threat of the snake being attacked by its food item will be nonexistent. Many a keeper has dropped a large rat or mouse into a king or milk snake's tank, left the room, then come back an hour later to find the snake chewed to pieces. But there is a valid argument to be made by the those who say live food is better— the snake never gets any exercise the rest of the time its in captivity, so

now that it doesn't even have to fight for its food anymore it will be completely lethargic. It's just like a cat that sleeps around the house all day—after a while you have to place its food bowl right in front of it. A few weeks later the cat gets up, takes five steps, its fatty heart seizes up like a car engine with no oil, and thud! It drops dead. Snakes need to keep that "killer instinct" alive or else they will simply become colorful ornaments that lie in glass boxes, unmoving. The bottom line is it's up to the keeper to decide what they want to do. There certainly is plenty of truth to the claim that a live food item can kill a snake, but this really doesn't happen that often and won't happen at all if the snake's keeper makes a point of staying around to supervise each eating session.

Q: What's the best way to defrost frozen mice and rats?

There are two good ways. The first one involves taking the rodent out of the freezer and simply leaving it in the open until it is fully defrosted. This may take some time but it assures that the process will be

Photo of a California Kingsnake, *Lampropeltis getula californiae*, by Isabelle Francais.

Some keepers prefer to give their snakes live rodents because then the snakes will get a little exercise. There is some sense to this—captive snakes often become obese due to lethargy (which is natural in the confines of a glass tank), and being given pre-killed food certainly doesn't help matters very much. Photo of a Gray-banded Kingsnake, *Lampropeltis alterna*, by Isabelle Francais.

complete. If you plan to feed your snakes during the night hours, take the food items out in the morning. Place them on a paper towel and leave them near a sunlit window or on top of a warm surface.

The second way, which is a bit quicker, involves immersing the frozen food item in very hot water. Boiling water won't be mentioned, it almost always guarantees full defrostation. This second, speedier method may not guarantee this, and a snake that consumes a rodent which is warm on the outside but still frozen on the inside may very well develop a number of gastrointestinal problems. In severe cases, death may result.

want to eat at night, or only during the day. You will have to experiment because each snake is different. In general, some species will prefer the privacy of the night hours, but many others are voracious, opportunistic feeders that will grab every chance they get to take down a meal. Of course, for all practical purposes,

King or milk snakes that eat only reptiles sometimes can be weaned onto mice by being given mice that have been 'scented,' i.e., have been rubbed on the body of a lizard or another snake. Photo of a Coastal Plains Milk Snake, *Lampropeltis triangulum "temporalis,"* eating a Five-lined Skink, by Mella Panzella.

necessary and in fact is quite bad. Simply run a tap until the flow gets hot. Fill a bowl to the rim and let the rodent soak in it for about a half an hour to an hour, depending on the size of the rodent in question. The reason the first method is preferable is because, as I

Q: What time of day is best for feeding king and milk snakes?

Unlike many other snakes, those of the genus *Lampropeltis* are not as sharply affected by the time of day in regard to their feeding schedule. Of course, the snake you have may only

the ideal time is that which is most convenient for you, the keeper.

Q: How often should I feed a king or milk snake?

Every fifth day is good, but keep in mind that this is an idealistic concept and not necessarily what your snake will allow. Snakes can be very strange in their eating habits—many will begin fasting for no apparent reason and then suddenly start eating again. This kind of sporadic behavior can be very stressful on the concerned keeper, but the rule of thumb here is that as long as your snake isn't sick and does not appear to be losing weight, don't be alarmed if it is not eating. Again, ideally speaking, a moderate-sized meal every five days is most desirable.

Q: How large of a meal should a king or milk snake get per feeding?

That depends on the size of the snake, of course. You must use your judgement here, but remember—don't overfeed! This is not only one of the worst things you can do to a snake, but sadly it is one of the things most often done. If you have a newborn Florida Kingsnake, *Lampropeltis getula floridana*, which is perhaps six to eight inches long and no thicker than a pencil, giving it two pinkie mice

per feeding is more than enough. Along the same lines, an adult of the same subspecies, which can reach about three and a half feet, shouldn't be given any more than

King and milk snakes like to drink and will do it often, therefore it is essential that they always have clean water. Forcing them to drink dirty water is a great way to get them sick. Photo of a Desert Kingsnake, *Lampropeltis getula splendida*, by Isabelle Francais.

three full-sized mice every five days. Just because they will take more doesn't mean you should give them more. They must be given enough to grow, but not so much to endanger

their health. Use your judgement.

Q: How long should I give a king or milk snake to eat a food item?

Normally about an hour, but in the case of frozen and thawed items you could conceivably leave the food in the tank overnight. The point is, dead items pose no threat to your snakes, but live ones do. Many snakes have been attacked and even killed by aggressive rats and mice that were running around a tank unattended by the keeper. That is why it is best to set a time limit under such circumstances. If a snake is truly hungry, it will notice a live item in its midst and attack it. If not, the item should be removed and tried at another time.

Q: Is there any way to offer a food item that will increase a king or milk snake's desire for it?

There are a few ways. One is to stick the snake in its hidebox, then place the food item in with it and close off the exit. If you decide to try this

Live food items should be left with king and milk snakes only for about an hour (and, in the case of food items capable of causing injuries, you should monitor the proceedings). If the snake doesn't show any interest after that time, chances are it isn't hungry. Photo of a San Luis Potosi Kingsnake, *Lampropeltis mexicana*, by Isabelle Francais.

with a live food item, be sure you remain close by and listen for any signs of trouble. Many snakes have a habit of only eating in situations where they have a great amount of privacy.

Another method, in the case of pre-killed items, be shaken up a bit in order to inspire a feeding response. Along the same lines, you may simply have a snake that only prefers dead food or vice-versa.

A somewhat grisly technique used by many professional keepers is blood is a strong stimulant and seems to trigger feeding responses in specimens that otherwise show no interest.

If you have more than one snake in a tank, that could be your problem right there. Many snakes

There are a number of techniques that can be used to get a stubborn snake to eat. One is to 'trap' the snake in its hidebox along with its food item. Another is to 'tease' the snake with the food item. Finally, there is the rather grisly but often effective method of slitting open a pre-killed food item and letting the scent of the blood and guts sort of 'seduce' the snake into a feeding response. Photo of a Scarlet Kingsnake, *Lampropeltis elapsoides*, by Suzanne and Joseph T. Collins.

is to tease the snake with the item by way of forceps. Push the item lightly into the snake's face and even tap it on the head a few times. Often a snake will become so lethargic in captivity that it needs to the cutting of the food item's body so it bleeds a bit. This is often used in the case of small snakes that refuse to take pinkies. What a keeper will do is take a small knife and cut the pinkie's head. Apparently the refuse to feed with others nearby. A separate feeding container is a good idea. Take one tank that is reasonably close in size to the snakes' main tank, and simply feed the snakes one at a time. Others things to

Often a snake's stubbornness to feed is caused by simple things, like the snake having too many cagemates, only being offered food during light hours, or being watched by the keeper when it would rather eat in private. Photo of a California Kingsnake, *Lampropeltis getula californiae*, by Isabelle Francais.

check for are a lack or overabundance of heat, too much or too little moisture, and other climatic factors that may be inappropriate for the snake you're keeping. The bottom line is, snakes often have feeding idiosyncrasies that will be difficult to discover. It is only through patience and experimentation that you will come to discover them, but keep in mind that even the most bizarre details should not be ruled out.

FEEDING PROBLEMS

Q: If my king or milk snake refuses to eat, what's wrong?

A lack of appetite can signal a number of things, but not all of them are bad. For instance, virtually all snakes have the habit of occasionally fasting for one reason or another. There are many factors that can cause this, but these don't matter to you, the keeper. What you have to do when your snake makes a break in its regular feeding habit is determine whether it is for a good reason or a bad one.

First, check its weight once a week. Is it dropping? If not, you probably don't have too much to worry about. If it is, chances are you have a sick snake.

Second, examine the snake's head and body for any obvious external signs of ill health. Are there any cuts or burns on the skin? Perhaps a sharp piece of the

Inadequate temperature often affects a snake's appetite. Even a normally voracious snake will stop eating if it becomes too cold because its metabolism will slow down to the point where it simply doesn't need to eat. Photo of a San Luis Potosi Kingsnake, *Lampropeltis mexicana*, by K. T. Nemuras.

Health problems will most certainly have a bad effect on a snake's appetite, so be sure to check for any outward signs if any of your snakes have stopped eating. Photo of a Mexican Milk Snake, *Lampropeltis triangulum annulata*, by K. H. Switak.

substrate has punctured the skin surface. Maybe you will detect a few ticks or a mite colony. On the head, you may find a remaining brille (eye cap) from a past shed, or perhaps the first signs of mouth rot are recognizable.

Certain climatic subtleties can cause a snake to stop eating. Severe temperature changes will almost always throw a snake off. If you have, for example, always kept the animal at 85°F and then suddenly dropped it down to 75°F, chances are the animal will not be able to adjust right away and consequently will not be thinking much about food. Along the same lines, if a snake doesn't have fresh water, is in a tank that's too humid, or is lying in a tank that desperately needs cleaning, then the answer to the problem will be right there. Poor husbandry is certainly a cause for an animal's lack of appetite.

If after close examination you decide your snake is simply on a fasting cycle, leave it be until it starts up again on its own. If you decide otherwise, then either refer to the disease section in the back of this book to see if there's anything you can do on your own, or bring your pet to a vet as soon as possible. Once a snake is sick enough to the point where it shows no further interest in food, then it is already in trouble.

FORCE-FEEDING

Q: When should I force-feed a king or milk snake?

Only as a last resort. If you have a snake that has not taken food in quite a while and you are sure you have tried every other means at your disposal to get it to eat on its own, only then should you resort to force-feeding techniques.

Q: What are the risks in force-feeding a king or milk snake?

Sadly, there are many. First, force-feeding itself is a fairly tricky procedure that the unpracticed hand could very easily turn into a tragedy. One main threat is damage to the snake's trachea. Other sensitive areas include the jaws and the outside of the head, which can be damaged by the keeper applying too much pressure.

Q: What is the best food to force-feed a king or milk snake?

Every fourth or fifth feeding, sprinkle a little calcium powder on your snake's food items; this will raise their nutritional value. Such powder can be found in most pet shops that carry herpetocultural goods. Photo courtesy of American Reptile.

There are two—a liquid mixture and a solid item. The liquid mixture must of course be fed via a plastic force-feeding syringe and usually consists of one raw egg, a very small amount of lean hamburger meat, and a pinch of multivitamin powder. These three items should be blended until liquefied, then run through a strainer (to remove any remaining fatty parts, which are not only no good for the snake but will also clog the syringe), then warmed to room temperature. This last step is crucial because feeding a snake anything too cold can cause it great harm. Liquid-feeding is best on smaller, more delicate specimens but can be used on larger ones if you prefer.

The solid food is usually nothing more than a small strip of raw beef, cut to roughly match the size of the meal the snake would take if it were eating normally. It is best to cut the beef strip a little smaller so it will be easier for your to slide it down the snake's throat. Meat strips are best only used on larger snakes since chances are you will have to do a little bit of struggling in order to get the snake to comply, and when working with tiny specimens the risk of injury is simply too great.

Q: What is the proper way to force-feed a king or milk snake?

Since there are two items that can be given during force-feeding (liquid mixture or raw meat strips), there are obviously two methods as well. In the case of the former, the first thing you must do is fill the syringe with the liquid. This is done easily enough by simply submerging the end of the tube into the liquid and drawing the plunger back until you have the amount needed. It is advisable that you always fill the syringe to its maximum; there are few things more irritating than going to the trouble of getting a tube down a snake's throat, emptying the syringe completely, then realize the snake didn't get enough so you must go through the whole process again. Once the tube is filled, squeeze the plunger down just a little so you remove any air from the tube. Now,

you have to get the tube down into the snake's throat, and this is where things can be tricky.

Before you do anything else, do yourself a favor and snip off the end of the flexible tubing at a sharp diagonal angle rather than a flat one. Since the end of the tube will then be pointed, it will be easier to pry it between the snake's teeth.

Now you can begin the actual force-feeding. Grasp the snake firmly with your thumb flat on its head and your other four fingers hooked under its throat. It goes without saying that you shouldn't grasp the animal too hard or you may injure it. Use your judgement to decide when your hold is tight enough. The remainder of the snake may thrash about violently (in fact, this will more than likely be the case), so you may want to either tuck the animal's body under your arm or, even better, if someone is there with you, have that person hold it.

Now take the tip of the syringe tube between the thumb and forefinger of your free hand, letting it protrude about one inch, and

carefully press the point between snake's jaws, preferably at the very back of the mouth. By pressing and turning simultaneously, almost in a "winding" motion, you can virtually always get the snake to part its jaws. When it does, seize the opportunity and start feeding the tube down into the snake's throat. Be sure not to push the tube too far down—it does not have to go that far. In fact, if you do push it too far you can very easily injure the animal. Depending on the size of the snake, a force-feeding tube only needs to go down about $1/20$ the length of the snake overall.

Once the tube is in place, you should then move up the fingers that are holding the snake's head just enough so you can close the mouth again. The reason for this is that if you allow the snake's mouth to stay open, it may very well thrash around until it slips the tube back out again. Don't close the mouth too tightly of course—if you kink the tube then you won't be able to squeeze the plunger.

Now that the tube is in place and held there

by the snake's own mouth, take the syringe in your free hand and *slowly* depress the plunger until you have given the snake the necessary amount. If you do this too quickly there is a very good chance the liquid will fill up in the throat and then begin overflowing out the mouth. This of course is not what the keeper (or the snake) will want.

Remove the tube slowly once the feeding has finished, but be sure to keep your grip on the animal because after such an episode it will probably be very stressed and thus very nervous. With your free hand, place the syringe carefully on the table or wherever you're working, gently grasp the rest of the snake's body, and carefully place the animal back in its tank. Release it slowly as well. Sudden movements on your part will only cause the snake to do the same, and when they start acting in this manner right after a force-feeding it often means they will regurgitate everything.

The method for feeding strips of raw meat to a king or milk

Force-feeding should be used only as a last resort. If your snake is refusing food, check other possibilities, those that are easily rectified, to find the root of the problem. Photo of a Honduran Milk Snake, *Lampropeltis triangulum hondurensis*, by Mella Panzella.

snake obviously does not depend on the use of a syringe. Here, you will need a pair of fairly long tweezers (forceps) that are not, repeat *not*, pointed at the tips. Since you will obviously have to place the tweezers into the snake's mouth, you don't want to run the risk of puncturing or tearing the inner lining of the mouth. There are a number of round-tipped tweezers that can be purchased at a surgical supply house, and they are not expensive. The idea is to open the snake's mouth, place the strip in the mouth, and get the strip far enough down the gullet to where the snake must swallow it.

Before doing anything else, make sure you have a bowlful of beaten and warmed raw egg yolk close by, as this is what you will roll the raw meat strips in so they will be lubricated enough to slip down the snake's throat. This is a very necessary step because trying to do this "dry" will very likely injure the animal.

In the first stage, the best implement to use is a thin strip of metal or tough plastic about the size and shape of a tongue depressor. In fact, there is nothing really wrong with using an actual tongue depressor but I choose not to because I am uncomfortable with the idea of sticking thin wooden objects into a snake's mouth.

As in the case of the syringe tube, the best place to pry the snake's mouth open with the plastic/metal strip is near the back of the jaws. Once the snake acquiesces, slip the bar all the way through until it is completely through the mouth and then turn it upward so the snake's mouth is opened at least half an inch. Again, hold the bar in place by gently

One easy way to avoid having to force-feed a snake is to make sure it's eating before you even purchase it. Photo of a California Kingsnake, *Lampropeltis getula californiae*, by Isabelle Francais.

Be careful when putting your hands near a snake after handling any of its food items. The snake may pick up the scent and bite you. Photo of a Gray-banded Kingsnake, *Lampropeltis alterna*, by Isabelle Francais.

squeezing the top of the snake's head and lower jaw. Then, with your free hand, grab the strip of raw meat and roll it once or twice in the warm egg yolk. Place as much of the meat strip into the mouth as possible, and then slowly and carefully remove the plastic/metal bar you used to hold the mouth open. If everything works correctly, the snake's mouth should clamp down onto the meat strip. At this point you will still be keeping your grip on the snake's head and lower jaw.

Take the forceps and grasp the meat strip on either side. Now comes the delicate part. While holding the snake's head firmly in one hand, gently push the meat strip down into its throat. It goes without saying that the snake will struggle in protest, so expect it. Once the meat is at least three-quarters into the throat, you can release the forceps, slide them back out, and use something blunt, like the eraser end of a pencil, to push the meat strip all the way down. Now that the hard part is done, all you need to do is place the snake carefully back into its cage and hope it isn't so annoyed that it throws the meat back up. Surprisingly, this doesn't usually happen.

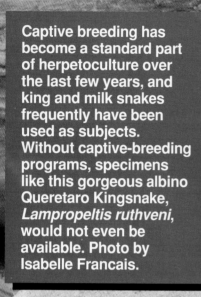

Captive breeding has become a standard part of herpetoculture over the last few years, and king and milk snakes frequently have been used as subjects. Without captive-breeding programs, specimens like this gorgeous albino Queretaro Kingsnake, *Lampropeltis ruthveni*, would not even be available. Photo by Isabelle Francais.

BREEDING

BASIC QUESTIONS

Q: Are king and milk snakes often bred in captivity?

Yes, very much so. They are among the most commonly captive-bred snakes in the world.

Q: What are the most commonly bred king and milk snake varieties?

The Sinaloan Milk Snake, *Lampropeltis triangulum sinaloae*, is very popular, as is the Gray-banded Kingsnake, *L. alterna*, and its relatives. Also favored is the California Kingsnake, *L.*

getula californiae, the Blotched Kingsnake, *L. getula goini*, the Scarlet Kingsnake, *L. elapsoides*, and the two mountain kingsnakes, *L. pyromelana* and *L. zonata* (although these can be very expensive). There are a few others as well.

Q: Are king and milk snakes difficult to breed?

No. In fact, they are probably among the easiest of snakes. This can be attributed largely to their high adaptability to captivity and generally calm nature.

SEXUAL DIMORPHISM

Q: Are there any easy ways to tell male king and milk snakes from females?

Not really, at least not any that will give you dependable answers, but you can still make good guesses. For example, it is generally believed that males have a broader tail than females, i.e., their tails do not taper off as quickly after the vent as those of the females.

Q: What is the most accessible method at an ordinary keeper's disposal for telling

One simple reason king and milk snakes are commonly bred in captivity is because they're usually very willing to do so. Photo of a Desert Kingsnake, *Lampropeltis getula splendida*, by Isabelle Francais.

male and female king and milk snakes apart?

A technique called "probing." In order to probe a king or milk snake, you first must have a surgical instrument called, unsurprisingly, a probe. The probes used in sexing reptiles look like thin steel rods with tiny spherical tips. There are a number of sources through which a hobbyist can obtain these, the phone numbers and addresses of which can be found through classified ads in the various herpetological magazines and society newsletters. Many pet shops also now carry these handy little 'tools of the trade.'

The probing technique is quite simple but requires a fairly steady hand. You must first coat the tip of the probe with some form of inert lubricating jelly. Then, slide it into the snake's vent on the extreme left or right side, and in the direction of the tail. Do this very gently and very slowly or you may end up injuring the snake. Also, you might want to have someone with you to hold the snake steady because, unsurprisingly, the animal won't care for this procedure very much.

Slide the probe in as far as it will go through minimal force on your part. If it goes in only a ventral scale or two then comes to a halt, chances are the animal is female. If it goes in farther, say five to seven scales, it is probably a male.

But again, and this cannot be stressed enough, this whole procedure must be handled very, very gently. If you don't think you'll be able to do it, find someone with experience and let them try instead.

HIBERNATION

Q: Is hibernation necessary with all forms of king and milk snakes?

Most, but not all. The few varieties that naturally occur in tropical regions will not experience any type of hibernation in the wild and thus do not need to be hibernated. However, it should be mentioned that the vast majority of *Lampropeltis* snakes that appear in pet stores and on breeder price lists are not tropical-zone species. They are, instead, of the cooler subtropical and temperate regions and thus should be "chilled" to some degree.

Q: Is hibernation absolutely necessary or can a king or

milk snake do without it?

Any king or milk snakes that you wish to breed (and, of course, which naturally occurs in a subtropical or temperate region) must be hibernated as the first step in the breeding cycle.

Hibernation acts as a catalyst for stimulation of the reproductive hormones. If a *Lampropeltis* snake is not hibernated it may still breed, but ninety-nine times out of a hundred the eggs laid will be infertile. This even applies to captive-bred and raised adults that have never been in the wild before. If the animal naturally hibernates in the wild, then it must be hibernated in captivity.

Q: If I am not planning on breeding a certain king or milk snake, does it still need to be hibernated?

No. In fact, many professionals prefer to keep their snakes active during the cooler times of the year in order to encourage an increased growth rate. This is done most often with newborns. Many will be of breeding size within two years as opposed to three or four. Of course, a king and/or milk snake is not going to breed until it is sexually mature, and that maturity has very

'Probing' a snake is one fairly reliable way of determining its sex, but the technique requires a delicate and practiced hand. If you've never done it before, learn from someone who has. Reckless probing can very easily injure a snake permanently. Photo by Isabelle Francais.

A nesting box should be provided for all gravid king and milk snakes. If one is not available, the mother snake will lay its eggs elsewhere in its tank, probably in an area that is too dry to support the eggs, and they will go bad. Photo of an Eastern Chain Kingsnake, *Lampropeltis getula getula*, by Isabelle Francais.

Once a king or milk snake has laid its eggs, remove the eggs as soon as possible. Some *Lampropeltis* eat reptile eggs, plus there is the danger of the mother snake moving the eggs around as she moves around. Photo of a Pueblan Milk Snake, *Lampropeltis triangulum campbelli*, by Isabelle Francais.

little to do with size. But studies have shown that snakes which are not hibernated during the first two years of their lives but instead kept warm and fed normally will be able to breed slightly earlier than those who experience more natural life cycles.

Q: What is the standard procedure for hibernating king and milk snakes?

First, you have to live in a geographic region where it gets cold enough for hibernation to take place. If, for example, you live a few feet from the equator, chances are you can forget about hibernating anything. If, on the other hand, you come from a place in the midwestern United States (like I do), then you will undoubtedly be familiar with a season known as winter. As long as you can provide steady temperatures of around 50 to 55°F for two months or so, your snakes will be able to

hibernate.

The next step is to set an initiation date. What day do you want to start hibernating your snakes? Be reasonable about your decision, remembering that the cold spell has to be sustained for about eight weeks. Obviously, the earlier the better.

Two weeks before the chosen day arrives, you should stop feeding the snakes you are planning to hibernate. There is a very good reason for

Snakes from the more southerly regions of the king and milk snake range, such as these mating San Luis Potosi Kingsnakes, *Lampropeltis mexicana*, do not need to be hibernated at temperatures as low as those required for king and milk snakes that live in the north. Photo by Isabelle Francais.

this—if a snake goes into hibernation with any food in its system, the snake's reduced metabolic rate will cause the food to ferment rather than be passed, rotting in the intestines and killing the snake. As an added measure of security, you should also give the snake(s) a three-hour warm-water bath every day during the last three days before the chosen date arrives. This will help loosen and flush out the last of any remaining wastes.

Now you must set up the hibernation chamber. It need not be elaborate—in reality any glass aquarium will do. There should be a thick layer of soft substrate (soil or wood shavings do well) and perhaps a piece of cardboard for them to hide under (some people like to use towels, which the snakes can simply snuggle into.) A water bowl is also useful, as even hibernating snakes may want to takes sips every now and then (yes, hibernating snakes do indeed move around a little bit.) Naturally you will want to put a locked top on the tank for security. Also, you will need a small thermometer for each cage. It is imperative that you closely monitor

the temperature. Although the gradient for king and milk snake hibernation is fairly broad, you should still rely wholly on facts rather than guesswork. Be *sure* what the temperature is—don't assume.

Some king and milk snakes will appreciate the inclusion of a sturdy branch or two for climbing purposes. Photo courtesy of Penn Plax.

Multiple king and milk snakes can be hibernated together, but it should be noted that for safety's sake you should only hibernate specimens of similar size. And just for the heck of it, hibernate the males and females separately.

Now that you have set up the hibernation tank(s), you can place the snakes inside. It should be stressed, however, that the ambient temperature should be reduced gradually rather than abruptly or else the animals will go into shock, and some may very well die. By gradually I mean five to ten degrees each day until the ideal temperature is reached. For virtually all king and milk snake species and subspecies that should be hibernated, the magic number seems to be somewhere between 53 and 57°F.

If you feel the chamber you are planning to keep them in will be too cold, you should include a small thermostat-controlled heater, setting it to the desired temperature. Such heaters can be purchased at most any hardware or department store, and if you already own a heater but it does not have a built-in thermostat, there are external thermostats that can be purchased as well. Once you have placed your king and milk snakes in their "hibernaculum," and the process has officially begun, leave them alone. Disturbing them is only going to cause them great stress and in the process reduce their resistance to the rigors of their winter rest. Don't kid yourself—hibernation is very demanding on snakes, and the last thing they need is to see your face every other day. They must be kept in the dark, and in relative silence.

This is not to say they shouldn't be checked on. Once a week, take a flashlight (the lesser the wattage the better) and look into the cage(s) for signs of anything unusual. Has a water bowl been tipped? Is it empty? Does one of the snakes look like it is losing a lot of weight? If you feel you have found a problem, act upon it. It is no secret that many snakes die during hibernation in the wild. In captivity, conditions are of course more controlled, but there are no guarantees.

The ideal duration for king and milk snake hibernation is eight weeks. Even for the more northerly ranging species (which will hibernate for up to five or six months), eight weeks seems to be okay. If you want, you can always leave them in for nine or ten, but any less than eight is very risky. Some keepers claim they have achieved breeding results after only one

month's hibernation, but I do not advise or endorse this at all.

Taking king and milk snakes out of hibernation should be executed in the same way as they were put into it—gradually. Allow their temperature to rise over, say, one week, then replace them in their normal tanks (again, males and females apart, which is vital during this time) and begin offering food again about two days later. The reason for this two-day wait is because any snakes that have recently been returned to normal active temperatures will experience a short period of disorientation and food will probably be the last thing on their minds. Because of this, they will have reduced abilities to strike and kill food items and thus a rat or large mouse will become more of a danger to them than anything else. Also, some king and milk snakes may go through a shedding cycle after hibernation, so naturally they won't be able to eat until it is over—another factor of which the keeper should be aware.

After your king and milk snakes have warmed back up and begun eating they will, hopefully, be ready for breeding in

about two weeks' time.

MATING AND COPULATION

Q: When I put my two adults together in order to breed them, is it okay if I stay and observe?

Yes and no. It depends on the timing. The interesting thing about snakes that are locked in copulation is that they seem to go into some sort of deep "trance" during which time their attention is very hard to divert, but up until this point (during the period when they the two snakes are checking each other out and so forth) it is best to keep your distance. When they are finally mating, however, it seems they can be approached slowly and observed from a few feet away. In some cases the animals may not even acknowledge you until they're done.

Q: When I am ready to put a pair together, should I put the male in the female's tank or vice-versa?

For the sake of safety, put the female into the male's tank. I am making this claim purely from experience. I find that in the case of *Lampropeltis* snakes the females are often more protective of their own ground and thus a little more aggres-

When a female lifts her tail, it usually means she is ready to mate. Often a male has to go through some jerky stimulation movements to get her to this point, and sometimes she will not give in at all. Photo of San Luis Potosi Kingsnakes, *Lampropeltis mexicana*, by Isabelle Francais.

sive. I know of instances where females have actually attacked, killed, and consumed males who were trying to mate with them, but know of no cases of the reverse. Of course since king and milk snakes are notorious snake-eaters they should always be closely watched for any signs of cannibalism.

Q: How long should I leave a pair together who don't seem interested in each other?

No more than thirty to forty-five minutes to an hour. In cases where at least one of the two snakes is interested in breeding, you will see some sort of reaction within ten minutes. Perhaps a male will start rubbing against a female in an attempt to get her to lift her tail, or maybe a female will notice a newly introduced male and follow him about hoping him to do this. In such instances you should let events unfold and just see what happens. But, as I stated above, if no breeding behavior occurs within just under an hour, then chances are you'll have to separate the two and try again a few days later.

Q: When my snakes are copulating, I notice the male

biting the female's head and neck. Is this normal?

Yes. Sometimes during a mating a female will, for whatever reason, grow tired of the proceedings and decide she wants to leave. Of course the male, still attached, will become a little irritated and have to resort to some mild form of persuasion to calm her down and get her attention back. In the male's mind, that is what is being accomplished by this biting action. It is further believed that a male does this in order to hang on to the female while she moves about.

Q: How long does king and/ or milk snake copulation take?

Anywhere from fifteen minutes to an hour or two. There is no set time frame. In extreme instances it may take even more than two hours or perhaps only five minutes, but for the most part, a keeper can expect their *Lampropeltis* snakes to be locked in the act for about thirty minutes or so.

Q: Are there any special conditions I have to provide in order to get my king and/ or milk snakes to breed?

There are a couple of details that will be of great help, but most of

them can be realized by utilizing simple logic. They will need sufficient ground space. Let's face it—if you put two long snakes into a short tank, do you really think they're going to want to breed? Maybe if they're *really* worked up, but don't depend on such things.

A temperature that is too low will discourage two *Lampropeltis* from even looking at each other. Keep them warm—80 to 83°F. Coolness will slow their metabolism down to the point where their sex drive is literally paralyzed.

Minimize distractions. If you're thinking of having a few people over to watch the mating, make sure they stay far enough away from the tank. You may even want to cover it, then simply peek in every ten minutes or so to see what's going on. Loud music won't help, nor any other sharp sounds. Remember, snakes can't hear the way we do but they are sensitive to vibrations. Also, keep other snakes and food items out of the tank as well.

Q: Once a pair has bred, can I breed them again?

Sure. In fact, make a point of doing that. It is

of course a wonderful thing to be able to put two snakes together and have them breed, but you will increase your chances of success by getting them to mate again, and perhaps once more after that. If they are willing, there's no harm in trying it.

suffering from some other problem that has rendered him a poor breeder.

GRAVID FEMALES

Q: How long does gestation take with king and milk snakes?

Roughly sixty to seventy days.

nothing about them has changed at all. Others, however, will react very badly and forego food items altogether. It is nothing to be alarmed about unless the animal starts to look really bad, in which case you may have to resort to the dreaded force-feeding,

Breeding albinos to normally colored snakes doesn't guarantee albino offspring right away. It may take another generation of breeders to produce them. Photo of Queretaro Kingsnakes, *Lampropeltis ruthveni*, by Isabelle Francais.

Q: Is it okay to breed a male with more than one female, and vice-versa, during a season?

Yes. In fact, many keepers make a habit of doing this just in case one of their males turns out to be sterile or is

Q: Since my female has become gravid it seems she has lost her appetite. Is this normal?

Often it is. The stress of pregnancy weighs differently on each individual snake. Some will continue eating as if

which in the case of pregnant females is a truly delicate affair.

A final note that should be mentioned is that a large percentage of snakes that are perfectly willing to eat during gestation will in fact stop eating during the last week or so before they lay. If this is the case with one of your specimens, do not become alarmed.

Q: Can a pregnant king or milk snake be handled?

It shouldn't be. Handle such snakes only when absolutely necessary.

Q: I notice my gravid female being more aggressive than usual. Is this normal?

Yes, very often a pregnant snake will act quite nasty. It is simply a result of stress and can be quelled by giving the animal a little more privacy and basically leaving it alone.

EGGLAYING AND EGG CARE

Q: Are there any preparations I need to make when the time of egglaying draws near?

Yes. For one thing, you need to provide the female with a nesting box. A nesting box can be made of any number of things. A plastic shoebox will do fine, or a smaller glass tank. Whatever it turns out to be, it should be able to promote moisture retention and, of course, it needs to have a snug-fitting top. It should have only a moderate-sized access hole so as to keep out too much light, as this will afford the female added privacy, which she will appreciate greatly.

The box should be filled with one of two popular incubation mediums—granular vermiculite or sphagnum moss (some keepers like to combine the two). Both are moisture-conserving, relatively inexpensive, and can be found for sale

After laying her eggs, a mother king or milk snake may stay coiled around the clutch for a little while. She probably is trying to keep them warm, not protect them, so don't fear being bitten if you want to remove the eggs (although it should be pointed out that the female may be a little temperamental from stress). Photo of an Eastern Chain Kingsnake, *Lampropeltis getula getula*, by Isabelle Francais.

Most *Lampropeltis* lay a clutch of between five and 15 eggs, give or take a few, although young mothers may only produce three or four. The eggs will be elongated and white to creamy white. Photo by Isabelle Francais.

in places such as garden stores and home improvement centers.

A method I have used with success involves covering the floor of the nesting/incubation box with a two-inch layer of vermiculite, moistening it (only to the point of dampness, not sogginess) then, after the eggs have been laid, lightly draping a little sphagnum moss over the top of them.

Another detail to remember is the fact that a female will require a lot of privacy and thus should be left alone. As the expected laying date draws near you may want to cover the tank with a dropcloth or similar item.

Q: What should I do if I discover the female has already laid her eggs before I have given her a nesting/incubation box?

If the eggs have been laid in the female's tank somewhere, what you need to do is remove them and place them into a nesting box as described a moment ago. The eggs must be handled with the utmost care because they are remarkably delicate and can very easily be spoiled if jarred or jerked about. Also, they cannot be turned, either. The way they are laid is the way they must stay.

Q: If the eggs are laid in a cluster, should I separate them?

You should, but this is only possible within about thirty minutes after the laying takes place. After that time the eggs will dry together and cannot be pulled apart. Trying to do so at this point will undoubtedly cause some damage.

Any eggs that will not separate through gentle pulling will stay together until they hatch. It is of course best to separate them if you can, but if you really don't think it's possible, then don't try.

Q: I see an egg developing a light layer of fungus. Should I try to remove this, and if so, how?

Yes, any developing fungus should be removed if possible. One method is by applying a mixture of warm water and antiseptic mouthwash with a paintbrush. It is important that such fungus be removed immediately because if it is allowed to grow it will do so very quickly, and destroy the egg.

Q: How long do *Lampropeltis* eggs take to hatch?

The normal time is between sixty and ninety days.

Be very careful when handling king and milk snake eggs; they should always be left in the position in which they were laid. Photo by Isabelle Francais.

Q: What is the ideal incubation temperature for *Lampropeltis* eggs?

A safe gradient is between 70 and 85°F. Any lower or higher and you are in a risky zone.

Q: Are there any special preparations I need to make when the anticipated hatching date draws near?

Yes—you need to be sure the top of the nesting/incubation box is secure because newborn king and milk snakes are very tiny and can easily escape through even the smallest orifice.

Q: How can I be sure I know where the top of a *Lampropeltis* egg is, just in case it gets turned?

Just after the eggs are laid, mark the top of each one with a water-based marker.

Q: If an egg gets turned, is it automatically going to spoil?

Not necessarily. There have been a number of documented cases where a snake egg had been turned, then was quickly returned to its original position and eventually hatched without further problems. Don't discard *any* eggs until they have obviously gone bad.

CARE OF THE YOUNG

Q: What is the most common food for newborn king and milk snakes?

There are a number of things, and some of them, to be honest, may be very difficult for the average keeper to acquire.

Of course, newborn mice are the first items you'll try. They are, as you probably know, readily available in pet

Take measurements such as the weight and length of your snake's eggs every second week so as to gauge the eggs' growth progress, and record the information by writing it down in a journal or on a software program. Photo by Isabelle Francais.

stores and provide a good meal for your snakes. If they don't do the trick, tiny lizards are the next best thing. They are harder to acquire, but *Lampropeltis* snakes often respond favorably to them.

If lizards don't work, try the next reptilian item—other snakes. If you can actually supply your neonatal *Lampropeltis* snakes with other smaller snakes, then chances are they will love them. Beyond these three things, it's really pot luck. Try anything at that point.

Although a mother king or milk snake may stay close to her clutch after laying it, she will not display any of this maternal-type interest in her newborns. When the young hatch out, they fend for themselves. Photo of a Desert Kingsnake, *Lampropeltis getula splendida*, by Isabelle Francais.

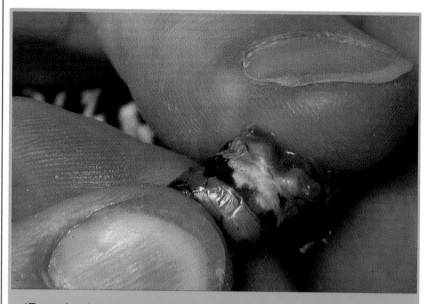

'Popping' the hemipenes is one way to determine sex in newborn kings and milks. However, there are some problems with this technique—you may injure the snake in the process, the results aren't always reliable, and the snake will become quite stressed, not to mention angry. Photo by Isabelle Francais.

Q: My newborn snake has been out of the egg for about five days now and still has not eaten. Is this normal?

It can be. Most newborn snakes need to shed one time before they begin eating. If it has already done that but has still not eaten, perhaps the problem lies in what food item you're giving it. Beyond that, you may want to inspect the snake's surrounding temperature, its cagemates (you might try isolating the animal) or perhaps the amount of privacy it is being given or not given. If the problem does not yield to these measures, bring it to a vet.

Q: I see an umbilical cord running from the newborn snake back into the egg. Should I cut it?

No! You could very well kill it if you do that. Just leave it alone and let it fall off naturally.

Generally speaking, when moistening vermiculite for use in snake-egg incubation, the amount of water you need to add should be equal in weight to the amount of vermiculite being used. Photo by Isabelle Francais.

Healthy king and milk snake eggs will be uniformly colored white or a pale, creamy white, like the one shown above. Bad eggs, however, like those on the bottom right, will be discolored and eventually develop a layer of fungus. Both photos by Isabelle Francais.

COMMON DISEASES

PLEASE NOTE—

Before going further into this chapter, I would like to point out that it is neither my nor the publisher's intention to suggest that the keeper try to perform any type of veterinary procedures on their own. There naturally are certain lesser actions that a layman can execute which will be of some help, and those are described in the text, but any type of advanced operations are strongly discouraged. Medical procedures with snakes are very delicate and require much knowledge, experience, and proper equipment. Therefore, it is highly suggested that you find a vet in whom you have full faith and trust. Develop a reliable relationship with him or her and use their services whenever necessary.

MITE AND TICKS

These are the two external parasites most commonly found on captive snakes. Either can come from a number of sources, but the usual one is exposure in the wild. Captive-bred snakes rarely develop a mite or tick problem, but when a keeper introduces a wild-caught snake into his or her collection without first quarantining it, the odds of a mite or tick colony infecting the other snakes is greatly increased.

Mites appear as tiny black dots moving about mostly at night, on both the snake's body and head. During the day they will hide under the snake's scales. If you view a snake with the light angle just right, you can see the silvery mite feces. Or, if you're willing to take the chance, you can simply pick the animal up and let a few crawl onto you. Mites are easier to detect when using white paper towels as a substrate, as they are so obvious on the light-colored surface. Mites almost always occur in large colonies, numbering in the hundreds and even thousands in very bad cases.

Ticks are a little easier to spot, since they only occur in small groups at most and grow very large. Even ticks that hide under a snake's

A king or milk snake that spends a lot of time soaking in its waterbowl should be examined for mites or ticks. Kings and milks are not very aquatic, and a snake suffering from external parasites often will soak to relive the irritation. Photo of an Eastern Chain Kingsnake, *Lampropeltis getula getula*, by Isabelle Francais.

You should perform regular checks for external parasites on king and milk snakes that are kept in highly naturalistic setups. Such setups offer mites and ticks plenty of camouflage, not to mention breeding opportunities. Photo of a San Luis Potosi Kingsnake, *Lampropeltis mexicana*, by Isabelle Francais.

scales will show eventually—they will attach themselves and suck so much blood that their bodies will bloat and make them conspicuous. Ticks usually find a home on a snake's body more often than on the head, although they probably have no real preference.

Both mites and ticks can be treated by a keeper in the early stages since no real veterinary work is required. With mites, the keeper should cut a small (about one inch square) piece of pest strip (small yellow bars coated with a mild insecticide) wrap it in fine mesh screening, then tightly staple the mesh to a small block of wood. The screening is used to prevent the snake from making contact with the strip.

Any snake that you've just acquired also should be closely examined for an ectoparasitic infestation. Many a collection has been ruined because one infested snake was introduced without first being looked over. Photo of a Gray-banded Kingsnake, *Lampropeltis alterna*, by Isabelle Francais.

Place the wood in the snake's tank (far from the water bowl) and leave it there for about five days. Then remove the piece for about five more days, and finally, return it for another five days to kill off any eggs or remaining mites. If this technique does not complete the job, you can soak the snake in a glass aquarium (complete immersion except, of course, for the head) in warm water for about five hours. Execute this method three days in a row. If any mites are noticed migrating to the head, simply wipe them off with a damp towel and dispose of the towel in a safe place. After each bath you should see dead mites at the bottom of the tank. I used this technique on a large specimen once, with superb results.

Ticks should be removed gently but firmly with tweezers, making sure the tweezer tips are as close to the snake's skin as possible (at the point where the tick has attached itself.) If the keeper breaks off only the tick's body but the head remains, severe infections could result. It should be noted that this method will very probably irritate the patient and should be handled by two persons in the case of larger specimens.

If the keeper feels uncomfortable with this method, he or she can try covering the tick with petroluem jelly. This will cut off the tick's oxygen supply, slowly killing it or at least giving it reason to release itself. Or, as with the second mite treatment, ticks can be drowned as well. Once a tick has been removed, swab the infected area with hydrogen peroxide once a day for at three days and watch the snake carefully for infection.

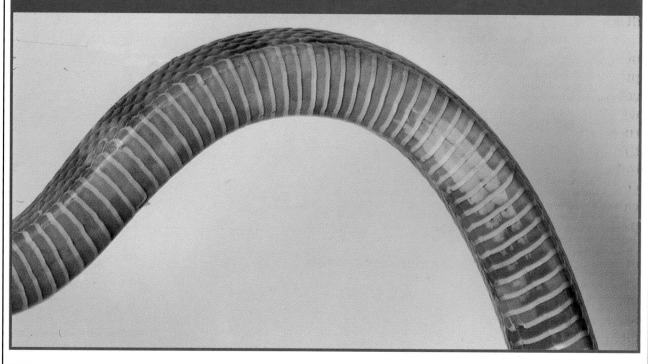

One of the favorite hiding places of mites and ticks (mites especially) is in a snake's belly scales. These scales are deep, tight, and readily accessible. Photo by Isabelle Francais.

Sometimes a king or milk snake will have trouble shedding its skin (which, ideally, should be shed in one complete piece). If that is the case, you can assist the animal by bathing it in warm water, then peeling the skin back by hand. Most importantly, you must remove the skin from the eyes (the 'eye caps'). Photo of a Honduran Milk Snake, *Lampropeltis triangulum hondurensis*, by Isabelle Francais.

BURNS

Burns can be the result of many actions, but probably the most common are close contact with light bulbs or hot rocks. Burns appear on the skin, either in welted, bubbling form or as simple blemishes, and will cause a snake great pain.

The keeper can apply any one of a number of over-the-counter burn ointments directly to the skin (a daily application, cleaned thoroughly the next day before the new coat is applied) but with the more serious cases a vet should consulted.

CUTS AND LACERATIONS

These are something a keeper should not treat, but instead leave to a professional. Causes of severe cuts and lacerations include fights with other snakes, rough activities during breeding time, and aggressive behavior on the part of live food items.

The most you can do is perhaps swab a small cut with some peroxide. With larger wounds, it is best to simply wrap the area with a sterile bandage and contact a vet immediately. Very often a larger opening will require stitches, so this is obviously beyond the scope of the ordinary hobbyist, and since infections can develop easily with severe cuts, the faster you contact a professional, the better.

EYE INFECTIONS

These manifest themselves in a great number of ways, such as swelling on or around the eye itself, actual bleeding around the eye, etc. The point is, eye problems simply cannot be effectively treated by an untrained hobbyist and are purely a vet's concern. Eye infections can be caused by many things, including dirty water, fights with cagemates or live prey items, too many rough objects in a cage, or complications from shedding.

SHEDDING PROBLEMS (DYSECDYSIS)

Probably one of the most common ailments suffered by captive snakes is shedding trouble. This manifests itself in a number of ways, but the most obvious sign is simply the skin that is still attached to the animal which should have peeled off.

The biggest worry a keeper should have with dysecdysis is the remaining eye cap, or brille. This is the most important part of a shed. While other parts of the body can retain the old skin until the next slough, a stubborn eye cap can cause temporary, and sometimes even

permanent, blindness.

If you have a snake suffering from shedding trouble, bathe the animal in warm water for about ten minutes, then remove the skin by hand. Ninety percent of the time this will cure the problem. If

There now are a few products on the market designed specifically to help snakes combat shedding problems. Check your local pet shop for the availability of such products. Photo courtesy of Energy Savers.

there are sections which still won't come off, dab them with mineral oil, wait a few more moments, then try removing them again. With the eye caps, you may need a pair of needle-nose tweezers, but if you don't have a steady

enough hand (and be honest about this), then let a veterinarian do it—poking the snake's eye out won't accomplish much. Again, with larger snakes you may need some assistance, but that is to be expected.

The best way to take care of this problem is to avoid it in the first place. Dysecdysis is usually the result of a keeper's failure to provide his or her snake with the necessary implements required for efficient shedding. A rock, a branch, and a water bowl are all essential during this time. The water bowl can be bathed in, allowing the old skin to soften. The rock will help "start" the shed, as the snake will rub its nose against the abrasive surface. Then the first few inches of old skin can be wrapped around the branch, making it easier to pull off.

It should be finally stated that any large regions of unremoved skin, particularly those around the eye and including the brille, which do not yield to the above treatments should be taken care of by a vet, not by the hobbyist.

MOUTH ROT/INFECTIOUS STOMATITIS

Mouth rot is

A note to all would-be herpetological photographers—a snake looks its best immediately after sloughing off its old skin. This beautiful Gray-banded Kingsnake, *Lampropeltis alterna*, for example, shed the day before this picture was taken. Photo by Isabelle Francais.

undoubtedly one of the most common infections that attacks captive snakes. A keeper can spot mouth rot in its early stages by the presence of small white spots around the oral cavity. If not treated, softened and necrotic (dead) gum tissues and loose teeth will result, which will of course cause the snake to fast, and eventually wither away. An obvious sign of mouth rot is a snake that constantly sits with its mouth open because closing it on the sensitive tissues causes too much pain.

Fortunately, a keeper can treat the infected area with a mild antiseptic, swabbing it twice daily until the infection has cleared up. Any dead tissues or very loose teeth should be removed, and the animal should only be offered fluids. After about a week the problem should begin to disappear, and a week or so after that the animal should begin eating on its own. If not, consult a professional for more intensive action.

SWELLINGS AND BLISTERS

Often you may notice on your snake a swollen area, whether it be directly on the skin surface or apparently under it, or a series of blisters. These can either be very simple problems, or a sign of much greater ones.

In the case of a simple blister, the keeper can puncture the site, drain the fluid, and swab the area with hydrogen peroxide once a day for the next three days. This can also be done with a series of smaller blisters,

Any kind of problems that a king or milk snake develops around the eyes should be handled only by a veterinarian. A keeper that thinks he or she can perform advanced veterinary procedures may end up doing more damage than good. Photo of a Guatemalan Milk Snake, *Lampropeltis triangulum abnorma*, by Isabelle Francais.

Respiratory infections often develop from enclosures that are too drafty or too moist. This is yet another reason why giving your king or milk snake the correct enviroment is so important. Photo of a Honduran Milk Snake, *Lampropeltis triangulum hondurensis*. Photo by Isabelle Francais.

although those that are extremely tiny should simply be covered with a mild skin cream. If the site continues to blister, a vet should be advised.

In the case of a swelling that seems hard or appears to have risen from below the immediate skin surface, actual surgery may have to be performed. Such an operation can be as simple as inserting a needle into the region and removing the fluids, or cutting into the animal and taking out the cyst or lump. Needless to say, treatment such as this should be handled only by a professional.

RESPIRATORY INFECTION

Unfortunately common in captive snakes, the causes for respiratory illness are varied. Often a keeper will allow drafts to blow through a snake room in order to keep the air "fresh." While these intentions are noble, they also promote simple colds and even pneumonia. On the other hand, keeping a snake's tank too warm will seriously restrict its breathing, giving it cause to wheeze and choke. Similarly, environments that are too moist or too dry in comparison to a snake's natural surroundings will cause problems as well. Proper husbandry is the ultimate preventive technique with respiratory illness.

Early warning signs include wheezing and sneezing, and off-colored discharge from the snake's mouth and nose. The animal will become lethargic and lose all interest in eating. Furthermore, labored

One early warning sign in a snake of a health problem is lethargy. Is the animal suddenly lazy and listless while normally it is alert and active? If so, it would be wise for you to play it safe and assume there is a problem. Photo of an anerythristic Louisiana Milk Snake, *Lampropeltis triangulum amaura*, by Isabelle Francais.

breathing can be clearly heard.

The extent of effective treatment on the keeper's part includes readjusting the animal's surroundings to better suit its requirements, and force-feeding it until a vet can be reached.

Fortunately, there are many effective treatments providing the problem is dealt with before the latter stages.

The only sure way to maintain your king or milk snake's health is to practice proper husbandry and bring the animal(s) in for regular veterinary checkups. And the easiest way to deal with a health problem that has already developed is to catch it as early as possible and deal with it aggressively and immediately. Photo of a Guatemalan Milk Snake, *Lampropeltis triangulum abnorma*, by Isabelle Francais.

INDEX

Acquisition, 4
Breeding, 39
    captive, 39
    conditions, 48
    egg care, 50
    egg laying, 50
    gestation period, 49
    gravid females, 49
    incubation, 52
    mating, 46
    sexual dimorphism, 39
Cage Maintenance, 19
    cleaning, 19
Climate, 14
Diseases, 56
    blisters, 62
    burns, 59
    cuts, 59
    eye infections, 59
    mite and ticks, 56
    mouth rot, 60
    respiratory infection, 63
    shedding problems (dysedysis), 60
    swellings, 62
Feeding, 21
    force-feeding, 32
    frequency of, 25
    mice and rats, 23
    problems, 30
    size of, 26
    time of day for, 25
Hibernation, 40
    procedure, 43
Housing, 8
    bedding, 12
    enclosures, 9
    hideboxes, 11
    rocks, 10
    tanks, 8
    tops, 9
    ventilation, 17
Shipping Costs, 6
Young Snakes, 52